East Beach, Cromer

Village Green and Staithe, Horning

Salt Marshes, North Norfolk

Horsey Dyke

NORFOLK

East Anglia is a region of immense variety and interest and nowhere is that rich diversity of landscape more apparent than in Norfolk. Here there are no dramatic features – no mountain peaks or towering cliffs – but there is still plenty to delight the visitor to this "Land of the North Folk". From the earliest times the area has been settled. Numerous prehistoric remains can be seen, perhaps most notable the vast flint mine known as Grimes Graves with 300 shafts dug by Stone Age man. Ancient roads such as Peddars Way and the Icknield Way cross the county. Here there were important Roman settlements and later the Normans built castles, churches and great religious foundations. Some of the earliest examples of brick buildings are found in Norfolk as well as the characteristic use of local flint for churches and cottages alike.

With ninety miles of coastline Norfolk is almost an island, cut off from Suffolk by the River Waveney and the Little Ouse and from Cambridgeshire by the Great Ouse and the River Nene. The coastline is ever-changing and numerous little villages which were once busy ports are now separated from open water by salt marshes and mud flats, many of which are now nature reserves. The Broads, that unique blend of river, mere and windmill, attract visitors in their hundreds of thousands in the summer months. There are nearly 200 miles of navigable waterways to explore studded with bustling riverside boating centres. When the people have left, however, the Broads are still home to a wide variety of wildlife. Some of the rarest birds in the country are found here and endangered species like the swallowtail butterfly flourish.

From the 14th century to the time of the Industrial Revolution, Norfolk prospered from sheep and wool. Many of Norfolk's splendid churches and great manor houses owe their existence to the riches which came from the wool trade. Later, when the centre of the textile industry moved to the north of England, agriculture took over as the main activity, one in which Norfolk is still pre-eminent. The county is intensively cultivated and the fields of golden corn studded with scarlet poppies are characteristic of the region. Here too are large areas of heathland, dark green conifer plantations, the blue of the sea and, most famous of all, the shining waters of the Norfolk Broads. With its blending of heath and marsh, woodland and wheat, ancient manor house and thatched cottage and above all its superb quality of light, it is no surprise that Norfolk gave birth to the great school of landscape painters known as the Norwich School. Founded in 1803, it is the only English group to compare with the great Italian schools of painting and the works of Crome, Cotman, Stannard and many others have preserved the Norfolk landscape for future generations in the way that Constable did for Suffolk.

NORWICH and the River Yare

A medieval city of great beauty, Norwich was once surrounded by a four mile long city wall, sections of which can still be seen. The Normans were responsible for building both the castle and the cathedral for which the foundation stone was laid in 1096. Surrounded by lawns and the tranquil cathedral close, this magnificent building is known for its extensive cloisters and its fine array of flying buttresses. The lofty tower with its slender spire rises to 315 feet and, among English cathedrals, is second only to Salisbury in height. The nave roof is decorated with a splendid series of bosses which tell the story of mankind from the Creation to the Last Judgment. The cathedral was built in local flint and beautiful white stone brought by boat from Normandy up the River Wensum to Pull's Ferry. This ancient gateway to the cathedral takes its name from an 18th century ferryman who plied across the River Wensum. The old ferryman's house stands next to a flint water-gate which, in the 15th century, guarded a little canal through which some of the stone used to build the cathedral was brought at the end of its long journey from France.

The majestic Norman castle with its fine 12th century keep is prominently situated on the highest point of the town. Used for more than six hundred years as a county gaol, it was greatly restored in Victorian times and now houses a museum and a world-famous collection of paintings by artists of the "Norwich School" including John Crome (1768-1821) and John Cotman (1782-1842). Norfolk's county town has a long and varied history which is reflected in its many interesting old buildings and quaint corners. A lively open-air market has been held continuously since Norman times and at one end of the market square stands the Guildhall which numbers among its treasures a Spanish admiral's sword presented to the city by Nelson after a victorious battle in 1797. Picturesque, flint-cobbled Elm Hill, in the old quarter of Norwich, is lined with charming timber-framed and colour-washed houses, many of them dating from Tudor or Georgian times, and is preserved much as it would have looked 400 years ago.

The city attracted many craftsmen, including Flemish weavers, during Norman times and by the 1400s it had become a major centre for the wool trade. The wealth which was generated by the success of the textile industry was instrumental in the foundation of many magnificent churches. Once it was said that there was a different church in Norwich for every Sunday in the year and more than thirty are still standing within the walls of the old city. Agriculture also flourished in this fertile area and with a network of rivers by which goods could be exported, the city's prosperity was assured.

Elm Hill, Norwich

On the outskirts of Norwich, the Wensum meets the River Yare, longest of the Broadland rivers extending over fifty-five miles from its source near East Dereham through Norwich to the sea. It flows through a number of attractive villages including Brundall – one of the oldest boat-building communities on the Broads. Here Norfolk wherries were built and more recently some fine racing yachts. The distinctive wherries, which traditionally had black sails on a hinged mast which could be lowered to pass beneath the numerous bridges, carried cargoes of coal, timber, grain or beet along the network of Broadland rivers. Although the last was built in 1912, they continued to work on the river up to the Second World War. Less than two miles down the Yare, two dykes connect the river with little Rockland Broad, a reed-fringed stretch of water which is as popular with fishermen as Rockland Staithe is with yachtsmen. At Reedham the river is crossed by a chain ferry, the only river crossing point for cars downstream of Norwich. With its river-side green and Ferry Inn, Reedham makes a pleasant stopping place for holiday-makers on the river. The pretty market town of Loddon stands on the River Chet, a tributary of the Yare. Once it was a port at which Norfolk wherries called as they carried cargo from one Broadland town to another. Now Loddon is a popular stopping place for the yachts and motor launches which leave the Yare to explore the attractive, wooded River Chet but it still retains much of its charming old world atmosphere.

Norwich Cathedral

Pull's Ferry, Norwich

Norwich Castle

Sunset over Norwich

River Yare at Brundall

Rockland Staithe

Reedham

THE NORFOLK BROADS

A fascinating mixture of natural and man-made features, the landscape of the Norfolk Broads is unique. It is made up of a network of meandering rivers, dykes and open expanses of water comprising twelve large and twenty-four small lakes or meres, known locally as "Broads". These were created in part through the silting up of the river mouths which caused the streams to flow more slowly and widen out into shallow meres. The digging of peat for fuel also played a part in the process. For many hundreds of years considerable quantities of peat were taken from the area until, some five or six hundred years ago, the diggings began to flood, creating the reed-fringed lakes we see today.

The most important Broadland rivers are the Bure, the Yare and the Waveney. With their principal tributaries the Ant and the Thurne, they provide nearly two hundred miles of navigable waterways. Thronged with sailing boats and motor cruisers for much of the year, they are now protected by the Broads Authority which controls 130 miles of waterways. For centuries artists have drawn inspiration from the Norfolk Broads and the area is a naturalist's paradise. The surrounding marshland still provides reeds for thatching. A familiar feature of the landscape is the windmill. Today relatively few survive in working order having been replaced by steam and electric pumps.

Wroxham was the first of the Broadland villages to cater for holiday-makers when a boatyard began to hire out yachts towards the end of the last century. It is now one of the principal boating centres on the Broads, providing for all the needs of holiday-makers. The fine old bridge, which was built in 1614 and later widened, joins Wroxham with its twin village of Hoveton. Horning, with its shops and cottages grouped around the green beside the staithe and its three riverside inns, is another popular port of call. The largest broad in the Bure valley, Ranworth, is divided into two parts: Malthouse Broad is much frequented by pleasure boats while Inner Broad, which is privately owned, provides a peaceful haven for wildfowl. The little River Ant is a tributary of the Bure and among the mills which border this delightful waterway is Hunsett Mill, an old drainage mill. At Ludham Bridge the river is thronged with all types of craft for much of the year.

A wide river flowing through some of the most open country in the Norfolk Broads, the Thurne is an ideal stretch of water for sailing and other boating activities. Conveniently situated on the north bank of the River Thurne, Potter Heigham is a popular centre. Hotels, shops and boatyards are all gathered around the famous medieval bridge which is more than seven

Horning Ferry by night

hundred years old. The central arch is so low that many boats have to wait for low-tide to pass safely beneath it. Owned by the National Trust, along with Horsey Mere and more than 2000 acres of the surrounding country-side, Horsey Windpump was originally built to help drain the marshes by pumping water from the dykes into the river. This fine tower mill continued to work until 1943 when it was severely damaged by lightning, since when it has been restored and is one of the largest mills remaining on the Broads. The largest of all the broads, Hickling Broad is a vast, shallow expanse of water, fringed with reeds. Because it is so shallow it is necessary for sailing boats to keep to a marked channel to avoid the danger of running aground. At the head of the broad is Hickling Staithe with its moorings, boatyards and picturesque waterside inn.

The town of Acle lies between Norwich and Yarmouth and there are moorings for boats at Acle Bridge, about a mile away. A little further down the river is the pretty village of Stokesby. It lies in a region of open grazing marshes with windmills dotted about the landscape creating a typical Broadland scene. For centuries an important fishing port, Great Yarmouth is now best known as a lively east coast resort. Boat trips along the River Yare and the Broads start from the town and the Yacht Station, situated where the River Bure meets the River Yare, is always busy with leisure craft.

Wroxham Bridge

Ranworth Church from the Broad

River Ant near Ludham Bridge

Hunsett Mill, River Ant

Potter Heigham Bridge, River Thurne

Horsey Staithe and Mill

Pleasure Boat Inn, Hickling

The Yacht Station, River Bure, Great Yarmouth

Evening at Stokesby

St. Edmund's Church, Acle

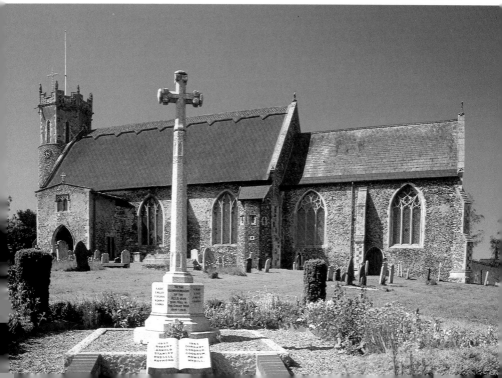

AROUND GREAT YARMOUTH

An ancient town which dates at least from Norman times, Great Yarmouth has for centuries been an important centre of the fishing industry, known especially for its herrings. An annual forty-day-long Herring Fair first took place in the town in 1270 and continued to be held for nearly five hundred years. There is still a busy commercial harbour providing safe anchorage for a variety of coastal vessels. The Maritime Museum on Marine Parade contains exhibitions relating to fisheries, lifesaving, shipbuilding and other aspects of the maritime history of East Anglia. A considerable section of the medieval town wall still survives and, between the wall and the river, houses were crowded into narrow alleyways known as "Rows". A few of these can still be seen as can the 13th century Tolhouse, one of the earliest municipal buildings in England. With the arrival of the railway in the 19th century came the tourists and a whole new leisure industry. Yarmouth developed as a popular family resort with four miles of sandy beaches, attractive parks and gardens and a variety of traditional entertainments and amusements. Britannia Pier is one of two piers in the town and at night the front becomes a blaze of coloured lights.

Situated opposite Yarmouth on the other side of the River Yare Gorleston, with its colour-washed houses and disused lighthouse, is a popular resort in its own right. The sandy beach is backed by the upper and lower esplanades which are separated by a wide expanse of grass. The Yachting Pool, located on the beach near the south pier, is much favoured by young visitors. Two and a half miles from Gorleston is the holiday resort of Hopton with the picturesque remains of an old church which was damaged by fire in 1865.

Just north of Great Yarmouth is Caister-on-Sea, a quieter resort than its lively neighbour although it was an important port in Roman times. It has a fine stretch of sandy beach backed by dunes and is also within easy reach of the Norfolk Broads. Surrounded by delightful country walks, ruined 15th century Caister Castle stands about a mile from the village. A short way along the coast is Scratby where the sandy beach is backed by crumbling cliffs which, like so many places along this coast, are constantly under attack from the elements. The low cliffs which extend from Caister-on-Sea along the coast to Hemsby are constantly subject to erosion and cliff top buildings have continuously been in considerable danger of crumbling into the sea. Hemsby has long been a popular venue for family holidays, offering one of the finest natural beaches on a coastline which is famous for its stretches of golden sand.

Britannia Pier, Great Yarmouth

Boats are launched directly from the beach in Winterton-on-Sea, a little fishing village where the sea makes its presence felt at every turn. Daniel Defoe, author of *Robinson Crusoe*, once visited the area in the 1720s and recorded that half the houses in the village were built using timber taken from wrecked ships. A memorial to the fishermen who have been lost at sea in the area can be found in the church which dominates the entrance to the village. Dedicated to the Holy Trinity and All Saints, Winterton church has an impressive porch paid for by Sir John Fastolf of Caister Castle. The fine 15th century church tower, which is constructed with knapped flints, stands some 132 feet high and is a landmark for miles around. About two miles inland is the attractive village of West Somerton. With its round Norman tower topped by an octagonal belfry, the Church of St. Mary the Virgin stands prominently up a steep lane to the east of the village. In the churchyard is the tomb of Robert Hales, the 'Norfolk Giant'. Born in the village in 1820, he grew to a height of 7 feet 8 inches and was once presented to Queen Victoria. West Somerton Staithe lies close to the coast road and footpaths lead inland from the village to Martham Broad which is also sometimes known as Somerton Broad. This peaceful spot on the River Thurne is managed by the Norfolk Naturalists's Trust and is an important breeding ground for birds such as the bittern and the harrier.

Marine Parade, Great Yarmouth

The Yacht Pool and Sands, Gorleston

The Old Church, Hopton-on-Sea

The Beach and Cliffs, Scratby

The Beach, Caister-on-Sea

The Sands, Hemsby

West Somerton Staithe

POPPYLAND

When the railway reached North Norfolk in the latter part of the 19th century, this coast with its clear light, invigorating air and unsophisticated charm had great attraction for romantic Victorian visitors. Entranced by the sight of all the wild poppies growing in corn fields and on cliff tops, they coined the name Poppyland for this newly discovered area. Around the turn of the century, the title came to be associated particularly with the area around Cromer, one of the least spoilt of Norfolk's seaside resorts, as a result of a series of articles which appeared in national newspapers.

Cromer is the principal resort on the North Norfolk coast and it is justly popular with holiday-makers for its fine beaches, bracing climate and splendid pier. The town developed originally as a fishing centre and is still the focal point of the local crab industry with the fishermen putting out in their brightly coloured boats each spring and summer to catch the crabs for which the town is famous. The pier, which dates from 1901, is a popular place for fishing, relaxing in the sun or visiting the theatre which continues to stage variety shows and concerts. Lifeboats have been stationed at the end of the pier since 1923 and one of Cromer's greatest heroes was Henry Blogg, coxswain of the lifeboat from 1909 to 1947. He was awarded the George Cross and four other decorations for saving life at sea. Alongside the Victorian hotels and boarding houses, the narrow, twisting streets of old Cromer are clustered around the magnificent 14th century Parish Church of St. Peter and St. Paul. Its massive 160 feet high tower is the tallest in Norfolk and from the top there are breathtaking views.

South of Cromer the coastline is studded with little coastal resorts, each with its own character and charm. Walcott and Bacton have become popular residential and holiday towns. Bacton-on-Sea is quite a long village, lining the coast road, and its wide sands are protected by groynes and a sloping sea wall. A cliff walk which offers fine sea views links Bacton to Walcott and at Walcott Gap the road runs along the sea wall with steps down to the sands. To the south stands the huge, isolated Church of All Saints, a well-known local landmark. Situated on a low cliff-top amidst cornfields and country lanes, Mundesley-on-Sea combines the pleasures of both coast and country. The wide sandy beach, backed by a small promenade, provides good bathing; inland the parish church combines architectural styles ranging from Norman to Perpendicular. A little way to the south of the village beside the road to Paston stands Stow Mill, a fine black-painted tower mill complete with sails and restored cap and fanwheel. It was built in 1827 and last worked in the early years of this

GT.Y.

West Runton Beach

century when it was converted into a dwelling. Heading northwards from Mundesley the coast road reaches the pleasant village of Overstrand. Here the gently-sloping sandy beach is popular with holiday-makers and there are bracing walks along the cliff top. St. Martin's Church dates from the 14th century when it was built to replace an earlier building which fell into the sea.

Between Cromer and Sheringham are the twin villages of East and West Runton, known collectively as the Runtons. Both have become popular little holiday resorts, each having its own sand and shingle beach under the cliffs with crab boats providing a splash of colour when they are drawn up on the sands. The old village of East Runton preserves its rural character with an attractive green, flint cottages and village pond. Sheringham, originally a fishing village well known for its colourful crab boats, became popular with holiday makers after the arrival of the railway in 1887. As the town lacks a natural harbour, the beach, which is comprised of shingle and gently sloping sand, offers a safe resting place for the boats when they are not at sea. Fishermen's Slope provides access to the beach from the promenade. Inland from Sheringham is the delightful beauty spot known as Pretty Corner. Surrounded by open, heather-clad countryside, it offers extensive views along the coast.

Cottages at Bacton

Paston Mill, Mundesley

The Town Sign and Gardens, Mundesley

The Beach, Overstrand

Cromer Pier from East Beach

Pretty Corner near Sheringham

East End Beach, Sheringham

HISTORIC HOUSES
Castles and Gardens

Among all the counties of East Anglia, Norfolk is outstanding for great houses including many which date from the 15th to 18th centuries and exhibit some of the earliest examples of ornamental brickwork.

Famous for its royal connections, Sandringham House is probably one of the best known of Norfolk's great houses. The beautiful wooded Sandringham Estate was bought by Queen Victoria in 1862 and the original house was replaced by an impressive Jacobean style mansion intended as a country home for the future King Edward VII. The house has long been a favourite private royal residence and both King George V and King George VI died here. The grounds, which are beautifully landscaped in the tradition of Capability Brown, contain lakes fringed by a mixture of native and exotic trees and shrubs.

Fifteenth century moated Oxburgh Hall, with its twisted chimneys, cusped tracery and mullioned windows of red brick, is one of Norfolk's finest manor houses. Standing a few miles south-west of Swaffham it was built in 1482 and has delightful formal gardens which include an ornate knot garden. The superb Tudor Gatehouse remains in its original form. It is probably the largest 15th century brick-built gatehouse in England, standing 80 feet high.

Among later Elizabethan and Jacobean houses, Blickling Hall near Aylsham is pre-eminent. Designed by Robert Lyminge and built between 1619 and 1627, it stands in beautiful wooded parkland and has some superb Jacobean style gardens. With its Dutch gables, turrets and clock tower the house contains some magnificent furniture and pictures. It is particularly known for its superb long gallery which houses one of the finest libraries in the country containing many rare early printed volumes. Hoveton Hall, with its superb gardens, is a more modest building but none the less delightful. Built in about 1700, it stands in the Broadland village of Hoveton St. John near Wroxham.

The 18th century produced several magnificent mansions including Houghton Hall, one of the finest examples of Palladian architecture in the whole of England. Lying a few miles to the east of King's Lynn, it was built for Sir Robert Walpole, England's first Prime Minister, in the 1730s and later embellished by the addition of domes and Venetian windows. William Kent was responsible for much of the interior design and many

Sandringham House

of the original furnishings and decorations remain, including some rare tapestries, Renaissance jewellery and fine 18th century book bindings.

Another fine Palladian building is Holkham Hall (1729-64), two miles west of Wells-next-the-Sea. Also designed by William Kent, it was built between 1734 and 1759 for the Coke family and under Thomas Coke, the great agriculturalist, the estate became very successful. Known for its superb Marble Hall and Statue Gallery, the house stands in a park landscaped by Capability Brown with a fine walled garden and a stable block which houses a collection of bygone equipment. Another well-preserved Jacobean mansion, Felbrigg Hall, stands just south of Cromer. It contains original 18th century furniture and pictures and one of its chief delights is its fine walled garden which originally provided fruit, vegetables and herbs for the household. The Hall is overlooked by a rare dovecote which once housed 2,000 white doves.

Surrounded by heathland and fine wooded country, Upper Sheringham is one of the loveliest villages in Norfolk. Sheringham Park and Hall were built to a design by Humphry Repton in 1812 and the imposing All Saints' Church contains a number of memorials to the Upcher family, for whom the house was built. Ancient oak, beech and fir trees grow densely in the park and in May and June rhododendrons and azaleas fill the woods with colour.

Oxburgh Hall

Blickling Hall

Holkham Hall

Felbrigg Hall

Houghton Hall

Hoveton Hall Gardens

The Temple, Sheringham Park

NORTH NORFOLK

Salt marshes, dunes and intertidal flats give the North Norfolk coast its distinctive character. So unspoilt and remarkable is this magnificent stretch of coastline that much of it has been designated an Area of Outstanding Natural Beauty and large parts of the coastal marshlands have been given over to nature reserves. Over the centuries many changes have occured along this coast. In some places the silting up of rivers has lead to once important ports now being land-locked, while in other areas erosion has caused whole streets and houses to fall into the sea.

Spread out along the coast road between Sheringham and Wells-next-the-Sea are several delightful little villages. Weybourne is thought to have been the site where the Angles, from whom the name East Anglia derived, and later the Danes, first landed. Picturesque Weybourne Mill is one of many mills which characterise the low-lying East Anglian landscape. A little further along the coast road are the villages of Salthouse, with its stone cottages, village pond and ancient church, Cley and Blakeney. In the Middle Ages before the sea retreated, Cley-next-the-Sea was a thriving port for the export of wool but now it stands half a mile from open water. The chief landmark in the village is its splendid 18th century windmill which looks out across the River Glaven. Blakeney was once the foremost port along the North Norfolk coast and although the estuary has silted up somewhat, it is still a popular boating centre. The harbour offers excellent sailing with safe moorings at Blakeney Quay and rows of dinghies are always to be seen drawn up on the Carnser, an expanse of shingle which forms the eastern bank of the channel. With its quaint, narrow streets and bustling quayside surrounded by merchants' houses and granaries, Blakeney is typical of the little villages along the north coast of Norfolk. The leisurely steam service provided by the North Norfolk Railway passes through beautiful coastal, woodland and heathland scenery along a line which was once part of the extensive Midland and Great Northern Joint Railway. It runs from Old Sheringham Station along the coast to Weybourne and inland to Holt, a delightful town which is largely Georgian in appearance since many older buildings were destroyed by fire in 1708.

Although it is now a mile from open water, the delightful town of Wells-next-the-Sea still has a thriving maritime trade and the quay is always busy with fishing boats and pleasure craft. Around the quayside is a maze of narrow streets and yards while boating activities are centred at the picturesque East End of Wells. A sandy beach lies about a mile north of the main town and can be reached by road or on foot along the sea-wall. Only a few miles from the North Norfolk coast, set amidst parks and woodland, is the beautiful village of

Blakeney Quay

Little Walsingham, its streets bordered by medieval and Georgian buildings. Possessing both an Augustinian Priory and a Franciscan Friary, Walsingham has been a place of pilgrimage for centuries. Traditionally, pilgrims travelling to visit the medieval shrine at Walsingham would remove their shoes at the Slipper Chapel at Houghton St. Giles and complete the last mile of the journey barefoot.

Some five miles away, situated on the River Wensum, is the attractive market town of Fakenham, a convenient centre for exploring North Norfolk. The delightful village of Burnham Overy is one of several villages in the area known collectively as The Burnhams. As the River Burn began to silt up, sailing craft were prevented from reaching Burnham Overy and so Burnham Overy Staithe was established a mile downstream. Although it was once a busy little port, like similar havens on the North Norfolk coast it is today linked to the sea only by a sandy creek running between saltings. Popular as a sailing centre, it is always busy with small boats and was once a haunt of Admiral Lord Nelson who was born in nearby Burnham Thorpe Rectory in 1758. Situated between Brancaster and Holme next the Sea is the delightful village of Thornham. Until Hunstanton developed as the major port in the area, Thornham had a flourishing coastal trade and the creek is still well used by fishing boats. The village boasts several old inns and an interesting church which contains a fine 15th century screen.

A typical scene, North Norfolk

North Norfolk Railway

The Mill, Cley-next-the-Sea

Blakeney from the Carnser

The Quay, Wells-next-the-Sea

Holkham Beach

Wells and Walsingham Light Railway

Common Place, Little Walsingham

Burnham Overy Mill

Burnham Overy Staithe

Burnham Thorpe Church

WILDLIFE
of the Coast and Broads

Although there have been immense changes in the landscape of East Anglia in the last fifty years, Norfolk still offers some of the most varied wildlife habitats in Britain including commons and heathland, the wetlands of the Broads, coastal salt-marshes and mud flats. Nature conservation has an important place in Norfolk for it was here that the first of the County Naturalists' Trusts was formed and many of the county's nature reserves are important national sites.

The combination of reed-beds, grazing marshes and shallow lagoons puts the coastal areas of Norfolk among the most important sites in Britain for bird watchers. The marshes around Cley-next-the-Sea are especially notable. Here bitterns breed and there is a growing population of avocets as well as a remarkable variety of wading birds. Sandpipers, redshanks, turnstones and sanderling are regular visitors who are occasionally joined by the rarer Kentish plovers and Temminck's stints. Fulmars and other sea birds nest on the chalk cliffs around Hunstanton and the nature reserves at Scolt Head and Blakeney Point are remarkable for their wildlife. At both places there are large colonies of terns, migrants are attracted here in the autumn and snow buntings are winter visitors. At Blakeney Point there are breeding colonies of both common and grey seals.

The Broads still provide a significant habitat for a variety of wildlife despite the increased popularity of the area for waterborne holidays with the resulting disturbance and pollution. Kingfishers, coots and swans are familiar sights on rivers and lakes while the marshlands of Hickling and Horsey are particularly significant, providing an important habitat for bitterns, harriers, bearded tits and the occasional osprey. Migrating birds also make landfall here. The last remaining haunt of the swallowtail butterfly is in the fens surrounding the Norfolk Broads.

Away from the water there are many other areas of exceptional interest for wildlife. Natterjack toads and nightingales can be heard on common lands, birds of prey spend the winter here and orchids grow in secluded spots. The pine woods, planted at many points along the coast to stabilise the sand dunes, provide ideal cover for birds such as blackcaps, goldcrests and redwings. The great houses of Norfolk also play a part in preserving wildlife. Herds of deer inhabit the parkland in which they stand and lakes such as that at Holkham Hall provide ideal conditions for flocks of Egyptian and Canada geese.

Coot

Swallowtail Butterfly

Mute Swan

Greylag Geese

Shelduck

Avocets

Ringed Plover

Little Tern

Common Seal

WEST NORFOLK

Famous as the east coast resort which faces west, Hunstanton stands on the Wash. The town is divided into two parts. The modern resort of New Hunstanton sprang up after the arrival of the railway in 1862 and has a splendid sandy beach beneath the cliffs. Unusually layered with red and white chalk and carr stone the cliff ledges provide a nesting site for a wide variety of sea birds. The ancient fishing village of Old Hunstanton lies half a mile to the north and its quiet little beach can be reached down a lane and across the dunes. Here among the mellow, red-roofed cottages and narrow lanes there is an impressive medieval church and a moated manor house which dates from the Tudor period. Hunstanton is known also for the fine parks and gardens which bring a splash of colour to the town.

The ancient seaside village of Heacham lies in a pleasant rural situation overlooking the Wash and is best known as the centre of the Norfolk lavender-growing industry. More than 100 acres is given over to growing varieties of lavender and herbs. In midsummer the fields are ablaze with rich shades of mauve and purple and the scent of lavender fills the air as it is picked and distilled to produce perfume and other products. The village itself, set among trees, has a pretty little green surrounded by old cottages and the beautifully-proportioned church is built of small flints.

Now used mainly for leisure pursuits, the River Great Ouse is a wide and attractive waterway which has long been an important thoroughfare. The ancient market town of King's Lynn is one of the oldest ports on the river. It was already a flourishing harbour at the time of the Domesday Book and by the 14th century it ranked as England's third port. Still a significant commercial centre, the town's prosperity is reflected in the elegant Customs House overlooking the Purfleet. Built in 1683 as a merchant exchange, it originally had open arcades on the ground floor. The beautiful Church of St. Margaret was founded in 1101 and the limestone for its construction was brought by boat from Northamptonshire along the Great Ouse. The church contains a remarkable Norman leaning arch but it is most famous for possessing the two best fourteenth century monumental brasses in the country. Opposite the church stands the ancient Guildhall. Erected in 1423, it is attractively faced with black flint and white stone in a chequer-board pattern. Some remnants of the city wall and the 15th century South Gate are all that remain of the town's medieval defences.

The low-lying East Anglian landscape is well-suited to windmills which have been a characteristic sight across Norfolk since medieval times.

Cliff top Gardens, Hunstanton

Although many were used to grind corn, others served as drainage pumps using the power of the wind to turn scoop wheels. One of Norfolk's finest mills stands at Denver just south of Downham Market. This superb tower mill, which dates from 1835, retains most of its machinery and houses a small museum in the original granary.

A few miles further north, near King's Lynn, is Castle Rising, one of the most picturesque villages in Norfolk. It is dominated by its ancient castle which is situated on a mound to the south of the village. Once of great strategic importance, the castle retains a fine restored Norman keep and some impressive earthworks. It was here that Queen Isabella, widow of Edward II, lived for thirty years after the death of her husband in 1327. The village of Castle Rising also dates from medieval times and was probably laid out about the same time that the castle was constructed, 1138. It retains many of its ancient buildings including a market cross, almshouses and numerous charming cottages. The Church of St. Lawrence, which has been carefully restored, dates from Norman times. Particularly noteworthy are the moulded arcade above the western tower arch and the triforium in the tower. Standing nearby on the green is a 15th century market cross and the splendid almshouses known as Trinity Hospital date from the 17th century.

The Beach, Old Hunstanton

The Green and Church, Heacham

Norfolk Lavender

St. Lawrence's Church, Castle Rising

Denver Mill

Guildhall and St. Margaret's Church, King's Lynn

BRECKLAND and
the Heart of Norfolk

In the heart of East Anglia, straddling the border between Norfolk and Suffolk, lies Breckland, an area which is unique in Britain because of its sandy soil and dry climate. Originally an area of vast heathlands, the landscape is now dominated by Scots pine and other conifers planted to help stabilise the light soils. Among the charming villages and bustling market towns found in the area is Thetford, an historic town which was at one time the most important city in East Anglia. In the 11th century the Bishops of East Anglia had their seat here and the ruins of Thetford Priory, a Cluniac house, can still be seen on the outskirts of the town. It was founded by the Norman warrior Roger Bigod in the 12th century and for five hundred years it remained an important religious centre.

North of Thetford, Swaffham lies in the midst of fertile agricultural land and in the 14th and 15th centuries a flourishing sheep and wool trade brought much prosperity to the town. One of the chief glories of the town is the 15th century church with its superb double-hammerbeam roof carved with angels. Its construction owes much to the generosity of local landowners and one notable benefactor was Swaffham's most famous son – John Chapman. Known as the Pedlar of Swaffham, and depicted on the town sign, he came into unexpected riches and paid for the building of the north aisle. At the heart of the town is the great triangular market place where a weekly market is still held.

Some four miles south-west of Swaffham, in an area which is rich in prehistoric remains, is Cockley Cley. Here is an Iceni Village and Museum, a reconstruction built on the site of an original encampment of the Iceni, whose warrior queen was Boadicea. Superbly situated near the River Gadder, the area includes a nature trail and a Saxon church which dates from AD 630 and is thought to be one of the oldest in the country. The remains of Weeting Castle, an early moated medieval manor house, stand near the famous Stone Age flint mines known as Grimes Graves. Rediscovered in 1869, this remarkable site consists of over 300 mine shafts with underground galleries. They were dug, using sharpened deer antlers, by Neolithic man about 4000 years ago in order to extract flints from the chalk beds below ground. The flints were then shaped and used as tools or weapons.

It is thought that the Romans may have used the ancient trackway known as Peddars' Way to keep Boadicea and the Iceni in check. Castle Acre is

Castle Acre Priory

situated where Peddars' Way crosses the River Nar and, because of its strategic position, it was a village of some importance from the earliest times. It was flanked on one side by a Norman castle and on the other by a Cluniac priory, both of them built by William the Conqueror's son-in-law. The houses and cottages owe their pleasing appearance to the blend of brick and flint, much of which was quarried from the ruins of these two buildings.

In the thriving market town of East Dereham, where author George Borrow was born and poet William Cowper is buried, stands Bishop Bonner's Cottage, an attractive early 16th century building which has some fine decorative pargeting. The Bishop was rector at the nearby Church of St. Nicholas in the 1530s and was notorious for his persecution of Protestants. North of Dereham is North Elmham, a village of considerable historic interest with a beautifully proportioned church, the remains of an Anglo-Saxon cathedral and a ruined castle.

The charming old market town of Wymondham is known for its abbey which has a somewhat unusual history. Following disputes between the monks of the Benedictine Priory and the townspeople, the abbey buildings were divided by the Pope who gave the nave, the north-west tower and the north aisle to the people of Wymondham. The monks walled off the remaining part and built an octagonal tower to rival the Great West Tower which the townsfolk built in 1445. Part of the abbey was destroyed during the Dissolution of the Monasteries but the buildings which remain are among the most outstanding in the county.

The ancient market town of Diss has a distinctive setting being built around a large lake or mere which covers some six acres. The narrow twisting streets of the town contain an attractive mixture of houses, shops and inns from a variety of periods. Half-timbered Tudor buildings with overhanging upper storeys stand alongside a wealth of Georgian buildings, including the fine Maltings. The attractive Shambles dates from Victorian times. There are several fine old inns in Diss including the timbered Greyhound and Dolphin Inns and the Saracen's Head with its traditional East Anglian plasterwork. The narrow main street is dominated by the Church of St. Mary the Virgin which has two notable chancel chapels built in the 15th century by local trade guilds. John Skelton, poet and tutor to Henry VIII, was at one time the rector of St. Mary's. Standing on the edge of Billingford Common about two miles east of Diss, is a fine example of a brick-built tower mill. This magnificent five-storey building, the last corn mill to work in Norfolk, has been fully restored and contains most of its original machinery. The boat-shaped cap, looking remarkably like an upturned dinghy, is a typical design feature which is found throughout East Anglia.

Thetford Priory

Weeting Castle

Iceni Village, Cockley Cley

A Breckland scene near Grimes Graves

Market Cross and Square, Swaffham

The Castle Ruins, North Elmham

Billingford Mill

Bishop Bonner's Cottages, East Dereham

The Mere, Diss

Wymondham Abbey

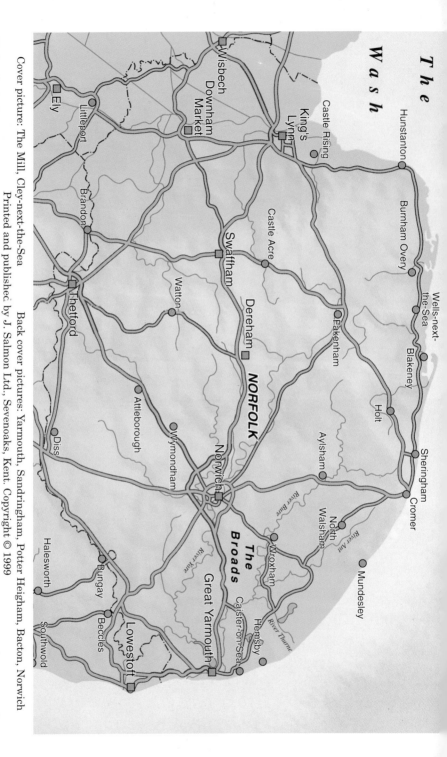